Contents

DIVE INTO THIS COMIC!

Get stuck in!

T0385994

Wilfred
and the Big Stick

3

The End

5

Where is Spotty?

Dan had pet bugs.

Oh no!

Oops!

Spotty is lost!

The End

What dogs like ...
by Wilfred

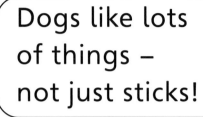

Dogs like lots of things – not just sticks!

Yum! I like food.

I like to play.

It's fun to run!

I like you.

I like you too!

It is fun to be with you!

I need a sleep now.

So do we!

Mmm... me too!

Zip and Zap and the Wet Stuff

Good! There is no wet stuff now.

It is good to be dry again.

Splash!

Spot the Difference!

Can you spot 5 differences?